Meditations for Great Lent

Meditations for Great Lent

REFLECTIONS ON THE TRIODION

Vassilios Papavassiliou

CONCILIAR PRESS ⋄ CHESTERTON, INDIANA

Meditations for Great Lent: Reflections on the Triodion
Copyright © 2012 by Theodore Christopher Vasilis
All Rights Reserved

Scripture quotations are taken from the New King James
Version, © 1979, 1980, 1982 by Thomas Nelson, Inc. Used
by permission.

Published by:
    Conciliar Press
    A Division of Conciliar Media Ministries
    P.O. Box 748
    Chesterton, IN 46304
Printed in the United States of America

ISBN 10: 1-936270-60-9
ISBN 13: 978-1-936270-60-6

Cover calligraphy by Jan Powell
Interior design by Katherine Hyde

Library of Congress Cataloging-in-Publication Data

Papavassiliou, Vassilios.
  Meditations for Great Lent : reflections on the Triodion /
Vassilios Papavassiliou.
    p. cm.
  ISBN 978-1-936270-60-6 -- ISBN 1-936270-60-9
1. Orthodox Eastern Church. Triodion. 2. Lent--Meditations.
I. Title.

BX375.T75P37 2012
263'.92--dc23
                        2012036498

Contents

Introduction	7
A Guide to the Season of the Triodion	10
1 → Humility THE SUNDAY OF THE TAX COLLECTOR & THE PHARISEE	13
2 → Repentance THE SUNDAY OF THE PRODIGAL SON	19
3 → Ascetic Love THE SUNDAY OF THE LAST JUDGMENT	25
4 → Fast from Sin MEATFARE WEEK	33
5 → Do Not Pass Judgment	41
6 → Forgive and You Will Be Forgiven FORGIVENESS SUNDAY	47
7 → Return to Paradise	51
8 → Passions and Virtues THE PRAYER OF ST. EPHREM	55

9 → The Virtue of Joy   73
CLEAN WEEK

10 → The Cross and Resurrection   77
THE SUNDAY OF THE CROSS

11 → The Canon of St. Andrew   83
CLEAN WEEK & FIFTH THURSDAY OF LENT

12 → Journey to Pascha   87

About the Author   91

Recommended Reading   93

Introduction

There is more to Lent than fasting, and there is more to fasting than food. This principle lies at the heart of the Lenten Triodion, the main hymnbook of Orthodox Lent. For the Orthodox Church, Lent is without doubt the richest and most distinctive season of the ecclesiastical year. The Lenten services, the spiritual lessons of the Triodion, and the biblical readings for the season invite us to simplify our lives and to immerse ourselves in the "bright sadness" of repentance.

Orthodox Lent begins on Clean Monday, seven

weeks before Pascha, when Orthodox Christians celebrate the Lord's Resurrection. But before Lent begins, it is announced in advance. This preparation for Lent is made above all through the Lenten Triodion, which makes its appearance in the liturgical life of the Church three weeks prior to Lent, on the Sunday of the Tax-Collector (or Publican) and the Pharisee. The Triodion remains a regular feature of the Church's liturgical life until the end of Holy Week.

Written for the devout Christian, the Triodion is full of warnings against pride and hypocrisy—the ultimate spiritual sins to which religious folk are so susceptible. Its hymns teach us the true nature and purpose of fasting and of Lent itself.

This short book gives us a glimpse into the spiritual depth and meaning of Lent. The chapters are divided into Lenten themes, each beginning with a hymn of the Triodion and followed by a brief commentary on each theme. Some of the

Introduction

themes are related to particular days or weeks of Lent and the pre-Lenten season (as indicated by the chapter subtitles), while others apply to the season as a whole.

A Guide to the Season of the Triodion

Sunday of the Tax Collector and the Pharisee (Beginning of the Triodion)

Meat Week (The usual Wednesday and Friday fasts Orthodox Christians observe throughout most of the year are suspended for this week.)

Sunday of the Prodigal Son (Second Sunday of the Triodion)

Sunday of the Last Judgment/Meatfare Sunday (Third Sunday of the Triodion)

Cheesefare Week (Fasting from meat only all week.)

Forgiveness Sunday/Cheesefare Sunday (Fourth Sunday of the Triodion)

CLEAN MONDAY (Lent begins). For the next forty days we fast from meat and dairy. Fish is permitted on the Great Feasts of the Annunciation (March 25) and Palm Sunday.

Wine and oil are permitted on all Saturdays and Sundays with the exception of Great and Holy Saturday (the day before Pascha/Easter Sunday).

Sunday of Orthodoxy (First Sunday of Lent)

Sunday of St. Gregory Palamas (Second Sunday of Lent)

Sunday of the Cross (Third Sunday of Lent)

Sunday of St. John Climacus (Fourth Sunday of Lent)

The Canon of St. Andrew (Evening of Wednesday or morning of Thursday of the fifth week of Lent)

The Akathist Hymn (Evening of the Friday of the fifth week of Lent)

Sunday of St. Mary of Egypt (Fifth Sunday of Lent)

Lazarus Saturday and Palm Sunday (End of Lent/Beginning of Holy Week)

HOLY WEEK (From the evening of Palm Sunday until Great and Holy Saturday). The rules of Lenten fasting apply also to Holy Week.

⇝ 1 ⇜

Humility

The Sunday of the Tax Collector and the Pharisee

Brethren, let us not pray like the Pharisee, for those who exalt themselves will be humbled. Let us be humbled before God through fasting like the tax collector, as we cry aloud, "God forgive us sinners."[1] (First troparion of Vespers, Sunday of the Tax Collector and the Pharisee)

*I*T IS NO COINCIDENCE that the season of the Lenten Triodion begins on the Sunday of the Tax

---

[1] All quotations from the Lenten Triodion are the author's translation, unless otherwise stated.

Collector and the Pharisee. Not only the hymns of the Triodion, but also the appointed Gospel and epistle readings for the season, play an important part in preparing Orthodox Christians for Lent. The lessons of the entire liturgical life of the Church from this point warn Christians to avoid hypocritical fasting, to fast spiritually as well as physically, and to abstain from wrongdoing, from pride, from judging one another.

The first lesson is the Gospel reading for the Sunday that begins the season of the Triodion:

> "Two men went up to the temple to pray, one a Pharisee and the other a tax collector. The Pharisee stood and prayed thus with himself, 'God, I thank You that I am not like other men—extortioners, unjust, adulterers, or even as this tax collector. I fast twice a week; I give tithes of all that I possess.' And the tax collector, standing afar off, would not so much as raise his eyes to heaven, but beat his breast, saying, 'God, be merciful to me a sinner!' I tell you, this man

went down to his house justified rather than the other; for everyone who exalts himself will be humbled, and he who humbles himself will be exalted." (Luke 18:9–14)

The main hymn for the day echoes the Gospel lesson:

Let us flee the proud speech of the Pharisee; and let us learn the humility of the tax collector, as with groans we cry to the Savior: Be merciful to us, for You alone are ready to forgive. (Kontakion for the Sunday of the Tax Collector and the Pharisee)

The warning to flee pride is given to us not only in words, but also in practical terms. On most Wednesdays and Fridays throughout the year, Orthodox Christians fast—that is, they abstain from meat and dairy, and usually fish also—but during the week following the Sunday of the Tax Collector and the Pharisee, these fast days are abolished.

Many Orthodox Christians make the mistake of thinking we are absolved from fasting during that week in order to gorge on meat and dairy before Lent begins, but this is not the reason at all. Indeed, if this were the reason, the Church would have appointed the following week—the week before Cheesefare week, when limited fasting begins—to suspend these fast days.

The reason the Church suspends fasting for this week is to warn us not to imitate the Pharisee, who boasts before God, "I fast twice a week." Thus the Church reminds us—not only through the lessons of the Gospel and of the Triodion, but also through its injunction not to fast during that week—that it is better not to fast and to be humble than it is to fast and be proud.

Thus the Sunday of the Tax Collector and the Pharisee gives us the first lesson of Lent: Physical fasting is a means to an end, not the end in itself.

1 ⇸ Humililty

If our fasting makes us prideful, we are better off not fasting at all.

Lent is thus announced as a quest for humility, which is the beginning of true repentance and the root and strength of the Lenten effort.

⇀ 2 ⇁

Repentance

THE SUNDAY OF THE PRODIGAL SON

Open to me, O Giver of Life, the gates of repentance: for early in the morning my spirit seeks Your holy temple, bearing a temple of the body all defiled. But in Your compassion cleanse it by Your loving-kindness and Your mercy. (Troparion of Matins, Sunday of the Tax Collector and the Pharisee)

IF THERE IS ONE CENTRAL THEME TO LENT, it is without doubt repentance. The season of the Triodion begins with the above hymn, which is frequently repeated in the period leading up to

Lent. We are thus reminded that the purpose of Lent is to return to God, not simply to change our diet.

But the theme of repentance—of returning to God—is made explicit on the second Sunday of the Triodion: the Sunday of the Prodigal Son. The Gospel lesson for the day is the following parable:

> "A certain man had two sons. And the younger of them said to his father, 'Father, give me the portion of goods that falls to me.' So he divided to them his livelihood. And not many days after, the younger son gathered all together, journeyed to a far country, and there wasted his possessions with prodigal living. But when he had spent all, there arose a severe famine in that land, and he began to be in want. Then he went and joined himself to a citizen of that country, and he sent him into his fields to feed swine. And he would gladly have filled his stomach with the pods that the swine ate, and no one gave him anything.
>
> "But when he came to himself, he said, 'How many of my father's hired servants have bread

enough and to spare, and I perish with hunger! I will arise and go to my father, and will say to him, "Father, I have sinned against heaven and before you, and I am no longer worthy to be called your son. Make me like one of your hired servants."'

"And he arose and came to his father. But when he was still a great way off, his father saw him and had compassion, and ran and fell on his neck and kissed him. And the son said to him, 'Father, I have sinned against heaven and in your sight, and am no longer worthy to be called your son.'

"But the father said to his servants, 'Bring out the best robe and put it on him, and put a ring on his hand and sandals on his feet. And bring the fatted calf here and kill it, and let us eat and be merry; for this my son was dead and is alive again; he was lost and is found.' And they began to be merry.

"Now his older son was in the field. And as he came and drew near to the house, he heard music and dancing. So he called one of the servants and asked what these things meant.

And he said to him, 'Your brother has come, and because he has received him safe and sound, your father has killed the fatted calf.'

"But he was angry and would not go in. Therefore his father came out and pleaded with him. So he answered and said to his father, 'Lo, these many years I have been serving you; I never transgressed your commandment at any time; and yet you never gave me a young goat, that I might make merry with my friends. But as soon as this son of yours came, who has devoured your livelihood with harlots, you killed the fatted calf for him.'

"And he said to him, 'Son, you are always with me, and all that I have is yours. It was right that we should make merry and be glad, for your brother was dead and is alive again, and was lost and is found.'" (Luke 15:11–32)

The hymns of the Triodion call Christians to identify with the prodigal, reminding us that we have squandered the gifts and opportunities God has given us on our own selfish desires. But all too often, Christians forget that this parable is not only one of repentance, but also one of forgiveness. There are two other key characters in the story: the compassionate father, a symbol of God the Father, whose readiness to forgive we are called to imitate; and the unforgiving brother, whose cold-heartedness we are warned to avoid.

The fatted calf that is slain for the prodigal represents Christ. We are thus reminded that Christ came into the world to save sinners. "I have not come to call the righteous, but sinners, to repentance" (Luke 5:32). During Lent, we must not be like the unforgiving brother, who observed all the father's rules but lacked compassion. Thus, we are not to observe the rules of Lenten fasting with coldness towards our fellow human beings who may not be fasting; rather, we are to be compassionate and welcoming to our brothers and sisters in Christ, as was the compassionate father. True repentance is the fruit of humility.

When we are humble, we judge ourselves and not our neighbor. That is why the theme of repentance follows the theme of humility.

The spiritual fathers of the Church teach us that we are to be hard on ourselves and easy on others. This is true humility; this is true repentance. We are invited to master this humility and repentance during Lent. Fast as rigorously as you can, but do not demand or expect it of others. If indeed we are all prodigals who have squandered the gifts God has given us, let us take further care not to squander the spiritual gift of Lent, which is an invitation and a means to return to God in humility and repentance.

3

Ascetic Love

THE SUNDAY OF THE LAST JUDGMENT

Knowing the commandments of the Lord, let this be our way of life: let us feed the hungry, let us give the thirsty drink, let us clothe the naked, let us welcome strangers, let us visit those in prison and the sick. Then the Judge of all the earth will say even to us, "Come, O blessed of My Father, inherit the Kingdom prepared for you." (Doxastikon of the Lity, Vespers of Meatfare Sunday)

ANOTHER THEME OF THE TRIODION, which naturally follows the theme of repentance, is the

Last Judgment. This is the theme of the third Sunday of the Triodion, just a week before Lent begins on Clean Monday.

The Sunday of the Last Judgment is known also as Meatfare Sunday. This is because it is the last day on which we eat meat before Lent begins. The following week is known as Cheesefare week, because during this week we eat dairy even on Wednesday and Friday (when we normally abstain from it) as we ease ourselves into the austerity of the Lenten fast.

But many become so obsessed with food as Lent approaches that they tend to ignore the connection between the Gospel lesson for the Sunday of the Last Judgment and fasting. On Meatfare Sunday, we hear this Gospel lesson:

> "When the Son of Man comes in His glory, and all the holy angels with Him, then He will sit on the throne of His glory. All the nations will be gathered before Him, and He will separate

them one from another, as a shepherd divides his sheep from the goats. And He will set the sheep on His right hand, but the goats on the left. Then the King will say to those on His right hand, 'Come, you blessed of My Father, inherit the kingdom prepared for you from the foundation of the world: for I was hungry and you gave Me food; I was thirsty and you gave Me drink; I was a stranger and you took Me in; I was naked and you clothed Me; I was sick and you visited Me; I was in prison and you came to Me.'

"Then the righteous will answer Him, saying, 'Lord, when did we see You hungry and feed You, or thirsty and give You drink? When did we see You a stranger and take You in, or naked and clothe You? Or when did we see You sick, or in prison, and come to You?' And the King will answer and say to them, 'Assuredly, I say to you, inasmuch as you did it to one of the least of these My brethren, you did it to Me.'

"Then He will also say to those on the left hand, 'Depart from Me, you cursed, into the everlasting fire prepared for the devil and his angels: for I was hungry and you gave Me no food; I was thirsty and you gave Me no drink; I was a stranger and you did not take Me in, naked and you did not clothe Me, sick and in prison and you did not visit Me.'

"Then they also will answer Him, saying, 'Lord, when did we see You hungry or thirsty or a stranger or naked or sick or in prison, and did not minister to You?' Then He will answer them, saying, 'Assuredly, I say to you, inasmuch as you did not do it to one of the least of these, you did not do it to Me.' And these will go away into everlasting punishment, but the righteous into eternal life." (Matt. 25:31–46)

What is the connection between this reading and fasting? The above passage tells us plainly that God will judge us by love, by whether we have, amongst other things, given food to the hungry. And here we can pinpoint one of the key purposes of fasting.

We abstain from food not simply as an exercise in ascesis, sobriety, and self-control, but out of love for others. Let us suppose that I normally spend x amount of money a week on meat. That amount I have not spent during the weeks of Lent I spend not on substitutes—not on gorging myself on delicacies which, while they may fall within the prescribed rules of fasting, betray its spirit and purpose. Nor do I spend it on other pointless luxuries I could easily do without—be it a film I want to see or a pair of fancy shoes to add to my already vast collection. Rather, I give the money to those who do not have food or drink or clothing or shelter. I give it to those who are in need.

Thus we see that our ascesis, if it is to be any kind of defense on the day of judgment, must be an ascesis of love. We deprive ourselves in order to have more to give to others. And if I as an individual am able through my own self-deprivation to help the life of another human being, imagine what a whole community, a whole nation, even the whole world could do if it observed such a fast!

Thus it is not a coincidence that Meatfare Sunday is the Sunday of the Last Judgment. We will be judged above all by our love—real, practical love—a love that is manifest in deeds and in sacrifice, not a timid, cowardly love that never dares to take a step beyond feelings and sentimentality.

Thus the Church again reminds us, in words and in actions, that Lent calls us to become better Christians:

> *Let us hurry to be cleansed through fasting from the stain of our faults and through mercy and compassion for the poor to enter the bridal chamber of Christ the Bridegroom, who grants us His great mercy. (First hymn of the aposticha, Vespers of Cheesefare Monday)*

Lent calls us to learn to love our neighbor as ourselves, and it does so not just in theory, but in practice. For through Lent the Church gives us a means of carrying out the commandment of love: by fasting.

⇾ 4 ⇽

Fast from Sin

Meatfare Week

In vain do you rejoice in not eating, O soul! For you abstain from food, but from passions you are not purified. If you have no desire for improvement, you will be despised as a lie in the eyes of God, you will be likened to evil demons who never eat! If you persevere in sin, you will perform a useless fast; therefore, remain in constant striving so as to stand before the Crucified Savior, or rather, to be crucified with the One who was crucified for your sake. (First hymn of the aposticha of the Praises, Matins of Cheesefare Wednesday)[2]

---

[2] Translation taken from *Great Lent: Journey to Pascha*, Alexander Schmemann, SVS Press (New York, 2003), p. 42

A FEW DAYS BEFORE LENT BEGINS, we hear this stern warning from the Triodion. Again we are reminded that fasting is not the be-all and end-all of Lent. If the fast is not a means to improving our spiritual lives, if we fast from food but not from sin, then we are no better than devils! The demons do not eat, but they are no closer to God for it. This is why, on Meatfare Sunday, we hear the lesson from St. Paul's First Epistle to the Corinthians, "food does not commend us to God" (1 Cor. 8:8). This is echoed in the Triodion:

> *The Kingdom of God is not food and drink, but righteousness and abstinence with holiness: and so the rich shall not enter it, but those who entrust their treasures to the hands of the poor. This is what David the Prophet teaches us, saying: The righteous man shows mercy all the day long; his delight is in the Lord, and walking in the light he shall not stumble. All this was written for our admonition, that we should fast and do good; and in exchange for earthly things*

may the Lord reward us with the things of heaven. (Eothinon, Matins of the Fifth Sunday of Lent)[3]

Being aimed at the devout practicing Christian, the hymns of Lent never cease to reiterate the warning Christ gave to His apostles: "Unless your righteousness exceeds the righteousness of the scribes and Pharisees, you will by no means enter the kingdom of heaven" (Matt. 5:20). We are not to fast for the sake of fasting. If our fasting is not aimed at making us better Christians, if it does not exceed physical abstinence, it is useless.

We already saw in chapter three how fasting can help us to be better Christians: we deprive ourselves to give to others. But Lenten fasting is not simply fasting from food. We must fast also from criticizing and judging others, from slander

---

[3] Translation by Mother Mary and Kallistos Ware, *The Lenten Triodion*, St. Tikhon's Seminary Press (South Canaan PA, 2002), p. 461

and gossip, from pride and vanity. Physical fasting is a reminder of and an aid to spiritual fasting. The Triodion spells this out quite plainly:

> *While fasting physically, brethren, let us also fast spiritually. Let us loose every knot of iniquity. Let us tear up every unrighteous bond. Let us distribute bread to the hungry and welcome to our homes those who have no roof over their heads, so that we may receive great mercy from Christ our God. (First troparion of Vespers, Wednesday of the first week of Lent)*

> *Let us observe a fast acceptable and pleasing to the Lord. True fasting is to put away all evil, to control the tongue, to forbear from anger, to abstain from lust, slander, falsehood, and perjury. If we renounce these things, then is our fasting true and acceptable to God. (First hymn of the aposticha, Vespers of Clean Monday)*[4]

> *Come, O faithful, and in the light let us perform the works of God; let us walk honestly as in the*

---

4   Ibid, p. 198

> day. Let us cast away every unjust accusation against our neighbor, not placing any cause of stumbling in his path. Let us lay aside the pleasures of the flesh and increase the spiritual gifts of our soul. Let us give bread to those in need, and let us draw near to Christ, crying in penitence, "O our God, have mercy on us." (First troparion of Vespers, Friday of the first week of Lent)

> The season of the holy Fast is now at hand. Let us begin it with good actions; for it is said, fast not for strife and debate. (Second Canon of Clean Monday)[5]

These hymns are inspired by a stern warning given to us in the Old Testament:

> "Indeed you fast for strife and debate,
> And to strike with the fist of wickedness.
> You will not fast as you do this day,
> To make your voice heard on high.
> Is it a fast that I have chosen,

---

[5] Ibid, p. 194

A day for a man to afflict his soul?
Is it to bow down his head like a bulrush,
And to spread out sackcloth and ashes?
Would you call this a fast,
And an acceptable day to the Lord?

"Is this not the fast that I have chosen:
To loose the bonds of wickedness,
To undo the heavy burdens,
To let the oppressed go free,
And that you break every yoke?
Is it not to share your bread with the hungry,
And that you bring to your house the poor who
   are cast out;
When you see the naked, that you cover him,
And not hide yourself from your own flesh?"
(Isaiah 58:4–7)

Thus we must not restrict our abstinence to food alone. In fact, we are better off observing a spiritual fast and not abstaining from food at all than we are observing the physical fast and ignoring the command to abstain from sin. Best of all, of course, is to observe both the spiritual and physical fast of Lent. "These you ought to have done, without leaving the others undone" (Luke 11:42).

That is what the Triodion invites us to do, that we may offer our whole being, body and soul, to God, that we may be temples of the Holy Spirit. But above all, we must take care to fast from the leaven of the Pharisees, which is hypocrisy (Matt. 16:5–12).

↛ 5 ↚

Do Not Pass Judgment

Consider well, my soul: do you fast? Do not despise your neighbor. Do you abstain from food? Do not condemn your brother. (Fourth troparion of the Praises, Matins of Meatfare Sunday)

IT IS SIGNIFICANT THAT THE DAY before Lent begins (Cheesefare/Forgiveness Sunday) we hear this lesson from St. Paul's Epistle:

Let not him who eats despise him who does not eat, and let not him who does not eat judge

> him who eats; for God has received him. Who are you to judge another's servant? To his own master he stands or falls. Indeed, he will be made to stand, for God is able to make him stand. (Rom. 14:3–4)

This reading was selected for this day to remind Christians that while the Church offers a general rule of fasting to all (no meat, no dairy, and most of the time no fish, wine, or oil), it is not realistic to expect everyone to be able to fast with the same rigor. Different conditions of life and health play a part in one's ascetic effort. What is important is not how rigorously we fast, but to what extent, if any, fasting improves our spiritual life, and whether we fast according to our own strength and ability.

An elderly woman with many health problems cannot fast as rigorously as a young man in the peak of his physical condition, but that does not make the former's fasting less valuable than the latter's. The old woman may fast only from meat, while the young man abstains from dairy and fish also. But the old woman eats frugally and simply, gives what little money she has to the poor, spends many hours praying, and does not criticize or judge others. The young man, on the other hand, while observing the dietary rules of the fast, gorges on soya cheese, crab, prawns, and the like,[6] spends money on himself rather than giving to others, and yet criticizes others for not fasting. Such a "fast" serves no spiritual purpose at all.

Therefore, the Triodion again gives us a stern warning about passing judgment on those who do not fast or who fast less rigorously than we. If we find ourselves passing judgment as the Pharisee did on the tax collector, then we fast in vain. For we have not even begun to fast from

---

[6] Shellfish is not prohibited by the fasts of the Orthodox Church.

the root of all sin, which is pride. Pride renders fasting useless. For there is no other way to know God than to humble oneself before Him. As C. S. Lewis astutely remarked, "A proud man is always looking down on things and people, and, of course, as long as you are looking down, you cannot see something that is above you."[7]

Lent calls us to stop looking down on others and to start looking up to God. But the image of a humble man in most people's minds is someone who is downtrodden. Indeed, this is the picture we are given of the tax collector, as we saw in chapter one. But spiritually and inwardly, the humble man looks up to God because, despite his penitence and contrition, he has hope that God will forgive him and accept him.

Therein lies the true meaning of repentance. It looks forward and not back; it looks upward and not down. It is, ultimately, something that

---

[7] *Mere Christianity*, Harper Collins (2002), p. 124.

leads us to joy and liberation. God calls us to true joy and true freedom, and we cannot attain that until we have rejected the false joy and freedom of sin.

⇝ 6 ⇜

Forgive and You Will Be Forgiven

FORGIVENESS SUNDAY

Let us all make haste to humble the flesh by abstinence, as we set out upon the God-given course of the holy Fast; and with prayers and tears let us seek our Lord and Savior. Laying aside all memories of evil, let us cry aloud, "We have sinned against You, Christ our King; save us like the people of Nineveh in days of old, and in Your compassion make us sharers in Your heavenly Kingdom." (First troparion of Vespers, Forgiveness Sunday)

*T*HE DAY BEFORE LENT is Forgiveness Sunday, when we hear this Gospel lesson:

> "If you forgive men their trespasses, your heavenly Father will also forgive you. But if you do not forgive men their trespasses, neither will your Father forgive your trespasses" (Matt. 6:14–15).

Fasting is not exclusive to Christianity. People of other religions and even of no religion also fast or abstain from certain foods for a variety of reasons, and many of them fast more rigorously than we do. If Lent is to be a truly Christian fast, it must be accompanied by love and forgiveness. Thus, before Lent begins, we are called to forgive everyone who has injured or offended us from the bottom of our hearts. Only then can we have a truly Christian Lent. Only then can our fast be pleasing to God.

The above hymn calls us to lay aside all

memories of evil. The memory of evils or wrongs (*mnisikakia*) is something the saints and fathers of the Church constantly warn us against. How often we hear people say things like, "I forgive but I do not forget!" Is this not another way of saying, "I forgive, but not really"? Surely, if we refuse to forget the sins committed against us, we have not truly forgiven them. We are still bearing a grudge in our hearts.

Forgiveness is intimately connected with the love of our enemies. We are to forgive our enemies, which means we are not to bear a grudge or hold their wrongs against them, we are not to return evil for evil; we are to show them mercy and compassion. This divine love and forgiveness is the imitation of God, and our Lord refers to it as spiritual perfection:

> "You have heard that it was said, 'You shall love your neighbor and hate your enemy.' But I say to you, love your enemies, bless those who curse

you, do good to those who hate you, and pray for those who spitefully use you and persecute you, that you may be sons of your Father in heaven; for He makes His sun rise on the evil and on the good, and sends rain on the just and on the unjust. For if you love those who love you, what reward have you? Do not even the tax collectors do the same? And if you greet your brethren only, what do you do more than others? Do not even the tax collectors do so? Therefore you shall be perfect, just as your Father in heaven is perfect." (Matt. 5:43–48)

Lent calls us to spiritual perfection, which is impossible without love and forgiveness. Thus, before Lent begins, we are called to forgive all those who have wronged us. Only then can we hope to attain perfection, which is the likeness of God.

7

Return to Paradise

Adam was driven out of Paradise, because in disobedience he had eaten food; but Moses was granted the vision of God, because he had cleansed the eyes of his soul by fasting. If then we long to dwell in Paradise, let us abstain from all needless food; and if we desire to see God, let us like Moses fast for forty days. (Third troparion of the Praises, Matins of Forgiveness Sunday)[8]

---

[8] Translation by Mother Mary and Kallistos Ware, *The Lenten Triodion*, St. Tikhon's Seminary Press (South Canaan PA, 2002), p. 178.

Another theme of Cheesefare Sunday is the expulsion of Adam from Paradise. The Triodion now brings us to the theme of food as a means of communion with or separation from God. Man's condition before the Fall was one of abstinence: "Of every tree of the garden you may freely eat; but of the tree of the knowledge of good and evil you shall not eat, for in the day that you eat of it you shall surely die" (Genesis 2:16–17).

Man lost Paradise by breaking this abstinence. Furthermore, man's diet before the Fall did not include animals: "And God said, 'See, I have given you every herb that yields seed which is on the face of all the earth, and every tree whose fruit yields seed; to you it shall be for food'" (Genesis 1:29).

Thus fasting is an invitation to return to Paradise, to man's condition before the Fall.

Fasting is also presented as a means of cleansing the eyes of the soul to enable us to see God:

7 ⇾ Return to Paradise

> *Moses was granted the vision of God, because he had cleansed the eyes of his soul by fasting.*

This refers to Moses' forty days and nights of fasting on Mount Sinai: "So he was there with the Lord forty days and forty nights; he neither ate bread nor drank water. And He wrote on the tablets the words of the covenant, the Ten Commandments" (Exodus 34:28).

We are reminded of this every week in Lent at the Liturgy of the Presanctified Gifts:

> *Almighty Master, who have fashioned all creation in wisdom, who through Your ineffable providence and great goodness have led us to these hallowed days for purification of soul and body, for restraint of the passions, and for hope of resurrection; who during the forty days put into the hands of Your servant Moses the tablets inscribed with divine letters; grant to us also, O Good One, to fight the good fight, to complete the course of the fast, to preserve the faith undivided, to crush the heads of invisible*

serpents, to be shown to be conquerors of sin, and without condemnation to arrive at and to worship the holy Resurrection. (Prayer Behind the Ambo)

The purpose of our fasting is spiritual. Spirituality must not be viewed as something that does not concern the body, but as something that is made possible through and within the body. We all too often find within ourselves a conflict between body and soul. The desires and needs of the flesh can all too often overpower the spirit. Fasting is a means of restoring the balance between soul and body, a means of bringing the flesh under the control and will of the mind and spirit. In restoring this balance, we turn back to Paradise, to the life of Eden. Then we can have hope that, like Moses, we too may see God.

⇝ 8 ⇜

Passions and Virtues

THE PRAYER OF ST. EPHREM

Let us set out with joy upon the season of the Fast, and prepare ourselves for spiritual combat. Let us purify our soul and cleanse our flesh; and as we fast from food, let us abstain also from every passion. Rejoicing in the virtues of the Spirit, may we persevere with love, and so be counted worthy to see the solemn Passion of Christ our God, and with great spiritual gladness to behold His holy Passover. (Second troparion of Vespers, Forgiveness Sunday)[9]

---

9   Translation by Mother Mary and Kallistos Ware, *The Lenten Triodion*, St. Tikhon's Seminary Press (South Canaan PA, 2002), p. 181.

At the heart of the Lenten effort is the struggle against the passions. The passions are spiritual or physical inclinations or instincts which, when uncontrolled, are destructive to both soul and body. Christian life is one of spiritual warfare against the passions, and during Lent, we are called to intensify our efforts in this war. The virtues are the positive counterparts of the passions, which Christians must struggle to attain and increase.

One of the weapons Christians have in this spiritual war is prayer. It is therefore no coincidence that during Lent Christians increase and intensify their prayer. During Lent, as well as during other periods of fasting, the Church increases the number of services. In Lent (ideally), Great Compline is held daily, and the Liturgy of the Presanctified Gifts is held every Wednesday and Friday. These services are unique to Lent, and through this Lenten worship we are able to participate in its "bright sadness," in the joyful repentance by which we are liberated from the mad rush, obsessive consumption, and thoughtless routines of daily life.

Of all Lenten prayers, one prayer holds a central position throughout the Lenten worship. It is known as the Prayer of St. Ephrem the Syrian:

> *Lord and Master of my life, do not give me a spirit of sloth, idle curiosity, love of power, and useless chatter. Rather grant to me, Your servant, a spirit of chastity, humility, patience, and love. Yes, Lord and King, grant me to see my own faults and not to condemn my brother; for You are blessed to the ages of ages. Amen.*
> (Service of Great Compline)

This prayer occupies such an important place in Lenten devotion because it sums up the very purpose of Lent and keeps us focused on our spiritual struggle against the passions. It is at the same time a prayer and a lesson. As we say this prayer day by day during Lent, we become increasingly aware that we are not acting upon it, and so our prayer becomes more ardent as it becomes more and more obvious that we need God's help to become better Christians.

The prayer begins by addressing some of the passions or spiritual illnesses that shape our life and character and prohibit us from true repentance. The passions mentioned in the prayer are four: sloth, idle curiosity, love of power, and useless chatter.

The first passion is sloth, which is, according to Fr. Alexander Schmemann:

> . . . that strange laziness and passivity of our entire being which always pushes us 'down' rather than 'up'—which constantly convinces us that no change is possible and therefore desirable. It is in fact a deeply rooted cynicism which to every spiritual challenge responds, 'what for?' and makes our life one tremendous

waste. It is the root of all sin because it poisons the spiritual energy at its very source.[10]

For as long as we are slothful, we will not make a beginning of repentance or of Lent. We will not bother fasting, going to church, giving time, money, and energy to others, or even praying. This is why it is the first passion addressed in the prayer.

Sloth leads to idle curiosity. Because we are spiritually lazy, not concerned enough with our own repentance and spiritual improvement, we become curious about everyone else's sins and shortcomings. This leads easily to the propensity for gossip and slander.

Love of power comes next. Because we do not accept God as the Lord and Master of our life, we wish to become the lord and master of ourselves and of others. We begin to see others as a means

---

10 *Great Lent: Journey to Pascha*, SVS Press (New York, 2003), p. 34.

to our own satisfaction. This can take many forms: desire for admiration, sexual gratification, financial gain, a sense of superiority, in which we see other people as necessary only to justify and glorify ourselves.

Finally, useless chatter. Words are powerful tools. They can bring comfort, illumination, laughter, joy, and healing. But they can also be very harmful. Words, when we are not careful, can wound, poison, and destroy. Therefore we are called to abstain from needless words during Lent, remembering the warning of our Lord: "But I say to you that for every idle word men may speak, they will give account of it in the day of judgment" (Matt. 12:36).

The prayer then turns us to four key virtues Christians should struggle to attain. During Lent, we are to intensify our efforts to acquire them: humility, chastity, patience, and love.

☙ Humility ❧

If pride is, as all Christian teachers have believed, the ultimate spiritual sin that blinds us to our own sins and shortcomings, then humility is the virtue that sees things as they really are. Therefore, it is only when we humble ourselves that we can make a beginning of repentance, for only in humility can we recognize our own sins. Thus humility leads to self-knowledge. But it leads also to the knowledge of God. Only the humble can see and recognize God, because God is Himself humble: "Take My yoke upon you and learn from Me, for I am gentle and lowly in heart" (Matt. 11:29).

☙ Chastity ❧

Chastity has come to be seen exclusively in sexual terms. But the true and full meaning of the Greek word for chastity, *sophrosini*, is "wholeness" or "wholemindedness." Chastity is therefore a state of being in which the soul and body work together as one. It is the harmonious relationship between the spirit and the flesh, wherein the body is under the control and will of the mind and spirit.

↣ Patience ↢

THE THIRD VIRTUE MENTIONED in the prayer of St. Ephrem is patience. Patience should not be understood, as it often is, solely in terms of waiting for something to happen—waiting for the bus or in a queue, for our exam results or whatever else. The Greek word for patience is *hypomoni*, which means "endurance."

The first form of patience—the ability to wait something out—is also an admirable form of patience, because it sees value in the waiting and not just the reward of what is expected. It is the patient man who will turn waiting for the bus into an opportunity for prayer, while the impatient man will get frustrated and bored.

But patience also means endurance. The greatest form of patience, and its greatest test, is patience in the face of suffering—the ability to endure wrongs and afflictions patiently. It is rooted in humility, for the humble man does not consider himself worthy of more than he receives. Patience understands that the here and now is not the be-all and end-all. That is why the humble man is patient with people. He knows that the person before him is not the whole being, not the finished article—just as a good teacher is patient with his pupils because he sees their potential, and knows that their knowledge or abilities will grow in time and with patience and effort. Patience is a truly divine virtue. God Himself is patient, because He sees all ends and knows the outcome of all things. The more we trust in God, the more patient we become.

↣ Love ↢

THE GREATEST of the virtues is love. We are told that God is love, and if we say we love God and do not love our fellow human beings, we are liars (1 John 4:20). But what do Christians mean, or what should they mean, when they speak of love?

There are four different Greek words for love: *agápē* (brotherly love), *érōs* (sexual love), *philía* (friendship), and *storgē* (compassion). The word usually used for Christian love—love for God and our fellow human beings—is *agape*. However, the other three words can also be applied to Christian love.

Philia

There is an interesting passage in the Gospel (John 21:15–17) when Christ asks Peter three times, "Do you love Me?" and Peter replies, "You know I love You." In the original Greek text, the first two times Christ asks, *"Agapas mé?"* The third time He asks, *"Phileis mé?"* as though He is asking, "Do you really love Me?" "Do you love Me as a friend?" *Philia* implies a closer, more personal love than *agape,* and our love for God should be that of a close, personal relationship.

Storge

Compassion is a form of love that every Christian should possess. The love the Good Samaritan showed to the robbed victim was compassion (Luke 10:25–37). The love shown to the Prodigal Son was compassion (Luke 15:11–32). Compassion is what moves our hearts to forgive and be merciful, to help those in need. God commands us to love our enemy. The love we have for our enemies is not philia or eros. Agape and storge are the forms of love we are to show to our enemies. We are not asked to like our enemies, to enjoy their company, to trust them. But we are to show compassion, to forgive, to be merciful, to see them as God's children and, therefore, as brethren. It is compassion that makes charity and kindness sincere. If we help others begrudgingly or bitterly, we are not really compassionate.

Eros

Eros is usually thought of as sexual or intimate love. However, it is interesting that some Church Fathers use this word to describe the highest degree of love for God. This is because eros is the most passionate form of love—it borders on obsession. Anyone who has been in love will tell you that they can't eat or sleep because they are in love, that the object of their love is the first thing they think of when they wake up and the last thing they think of when they go to bed, and other such things. Such should be our love for God.

St. John of Sinai (to whom the Fourth Sunday of Lent is dedicated), more famously known as St. John of the Ladder (Climacus) because of his famous work, *The Ladder of Divine Ascent*, says this is why so many of those saints who were once possessed by this passion of eros or its sinful counterpart, lust, ended up being those saints who most passionately loved God.

A great example of such a saint is Mary of Egypt (to whom the Fifth Sunday of Lent is dedicated), a wealthy prostitute who became one of the greatest ascetics of the Church. According to some stories about her life, she was not a prostitute for the money, since she was very wealthy, but because she enjoyed it. When she embraced Christianity, she gave up everything and lived a life of rigorous ascesis and penitence in the wilderness.

Such saints did not so much give up their passion as redirect it to God, replacing the object of their desire with God. This is a matter of great importance. Repentance is often thought of as a negative thing—as simply giving something up.

But repentance is in fact positive—it is finding the right and proper object for our passions. Our passions are in fact necessary; they are a gift. Without them we risk becoming lukewarm, indifferent, something Christ declares in the Book of Revelation that He detests: "because you are lukewarm, and neither cold nor hot, I will vomit you out of My mouth" (Rev. 3:16). The saints had a burning love for God. They were the most "passionate" people of the Church, but they directed those passions correctly, set them to their proper tasks and, with singleness of heart and mind, transferred them to one object of desire—that is, to God.

Agape

In terms of our love for one another, all four forms of love are good. But our love towards our fellow human beings is rooted in our love for God. Love for man in Christianity is not humanitarianism, which sees man as the supreme good and goal of life. Our love towards one another can often be distorted and sinful. Philia, eros, and storge, while in themselves good, can be perverted and exaggerated. This is why *agape* is the word most often used for Christian love. Agape is the purest form of love. It is love for all people. Love for one person that excludes love for others is not Christian love.

Love for friends (philia), for example, can lead us to show favoritism and partiality, to treat those who do not belong to our circle of friends unfairly.

Eros, sexual love, can be even worse, since it is the most passionate form of love and can even cause us to harm others. It can lead us to want to please the person we love at all costs. It can also lead easily to envy and possessiveness of the person we love. Its lowest and most distorted form is unbridled lust, when sexual gratification becomes the ultimate goal.

Storge, compassion, also needs to be controlled. Excessive pity for one person can cause us to overlook the needs of others. It can also lead us to spoiling others. This is particularly common in parent-child relationships.

Philia, storge, and eros are therefore to be directed by agape, by divine love. It is not that the other forms of love are bad and should not exist, but the objects of our friendship, compassion, and sexual desire are not to become goals in themselves. Love for God, divine love, is that which gives true meaning to all other kinds of love; in it they find their proper place and proportion.

Thus the spiritual struggle of Lent and of Christian life as a whole is not a matter of avoiding the passions, but of mastering them. This mastery requires discipline. This discipline, this mastery over the passions, is known in Orthodox spirituality as "dispassion" (*apatheia*).

It is regarded as an exalted state of virtue. It is sometimes misconstrued as "passionlessness," but this is not what it means. St. Isaac the Syrian says, "Dispassion does not mean no longer to feel the passions, but no longer to accept them."[11] Dispassion is harmony between body and soul. It is the attainment of wholeness or chastity.

This harmony is one of the chief purposes of fasting and asceticism. Thus our physical fasting is, together with prayer, one of our key weapons in the battle to master the passions and attain holiness: "This kind can come out by nothing but prayer and fasting" (Mark 9:29).

---

11 *Mystic Treatises*, ET Wensinck, p. 345.

↣ 9 ↢

The Virtue of Joy

CLEAN WEEK

Let us joyfully begin the all-hallowed season of abstinence; and let us worship with the bright radiance of the holy commandments of Christ our God, with the brightness of love and the splendor of prayer, with the purity of holiness and the strength of good courage. So, clothed in raiment of light, let us hasten to the Holy Resurrection on the third day, which shines upon the world with the glory of eternal life. (Kathisma of Matins, Clean Monday)

One virtue that for centuries Christians have been quite suspicious of is joy. During Lent particularly, Christians become very suspicious of this virtue indeed. In fact, it is often viewed as a sin rather than a virtue. Yet St. Paul includes it amongst the fruits of the Holy Spirit (Galatians 5:22).

Christians tend to think of Lent as a time of sorrow, but the above hymn refers to it insistently as a time of joy and brightness. Our Lord Himself reminds us that we are to fast joyfully:

> "When you fast, do not be like the hypocrites, with a sad countenance. For they disfigure their faces that they may appear to men to be fasting. Assuredly, I say to you, they have their reward. But you, when you fast, anoint your head and wash your face, so that you do not appear to men to be fasting, but to your Father who is in the secret place; and your Father who sees in secret will reward you openly." (Matt. 6:16–18)

This lesson is echoed also by the Triodion:

> *O faithful, with joy let us enter upon the beginning of the Fast. Let us not be of sad countenance, but let us wash our faces in the water of dispassion; and let us bless and exalt Christ above all for ever.* (Second Canon of Matins, Clean Monday)

Lent is characterized by what the Greek Fathers call *harmolypi* ("bright sadness" or "joyful sorrow"). This is because Lent, like repentance, is at the same time both sad and bright, both sorrowful and joyful.

Thus the purpose of Lent is to lead us into the joy of the Lord. The joy of which we speak is not the joy of the world, which comes and goes and depends on outward conditions. It is a deep, spiritual joy that springs from our loving relationship with Christ.

Those who think of Lent purely in terms of fasting and obligations can never fully experience the joy of Lent. The joy of Lent is offered to us in Lenten worship, through the services of Great Compline and the Liturgy of the Presanctified Gifts. These solemn services help us gradually to change our hearts and lives by entering into the bright sadness of Lent, through which we are able to make our own the joy of repentance, the joy of returning to God.

10

The Cross and Resurrection

THE SUNDAY OF THE CROSS

Having passed beyond the middle point in this holy season of the Fast, with joy let us go forward to the part that still remains, anointing our souls with the oil of almsgiving. So may we be counted worthy to venerate the divine Passion of Christ our God, and to attain His dread and holy Resurrection. (Third troparion of Vespers, fourth Sunday of Lent)[12]

---

[12] Translation by Mother Mary and Kallistos Ware, *The Lenten Triodion*, St. Tikhon's Seminary Press (South Canaan PA, 2002), p. 368.

*T*HE THIRD SUNDAY OF LENT is dedicated to the Cross. The reason for this is given to us in the Synaxarion[13] for the day:

> On this third Sunday of the Great Fast we celebrate the Veneration of the precious and life-giving Cross. Since during the forty days of the Fast we are also in a way crucified, mortified to the passions, contrite, abased and despondent, the precious and life-giving Cross is offered to us as refreshment and confirmation, calling to mind the Passion of our Lord Jesus Christ and comforting us. . . . Just as those who have traveled a long hard road, weighed down by the labors of their journey, in finding a shady tree, take their ease for a moment and continue their journey rejuvenated, so now in this time of the Fast, this sorrowful and laborious journey, the Holy Fathers have planted the life-giving Cross before us, for our relief and refreshment,

---

13 The Synaxarion is to be found in the hymnbooks of the Church. It provides an explanation of each feast day of the Church year and contains information about the lives of the saints.

> *to encourage and make easier the labors that lie ahead.*

It is clear, then, that the Sunday of the Veneration of the Cross is directly connected to our Lenten effort. If we have taken Lent seriously so far, by now we are probably feeling the strain of this effort. Our fasting is perhaps becoming harder to maintain, our acts of charity are perhaps dwindling or growing cold, sloth may be persuading us to stay at home rather than attend the evening Lenten services. We may be missing the worldly things in our lives that we may have chosen to cut back on or cut out altogether during Lent. And so the Cross is placed before us to remind us of the suffering Christ endured for us.

Furthermore, this day reminds us not only of the Cross but also of the Resurrection—the ultimate goal of our ascetic struggle and of the Lenten season—Pascha. The theme-hymns, or *hirmoi*, for this day all make reference to the Resurrection, and the canon for the day is chanted according to exactly the same melody as the canon of Pascha. Thus the Church reminds us, not only in words but even through melody, that Lent is the necessary journey to Pascha, and we cannot reach the joy of the Resurrection without going through the Cross. And so we hear in the Gospel reading for this day the words of our Lord: "If anyone desires to come after Me, let him deny himself, and take up his cross, and follow Me" (Matt. 16:24).

The Cross and Resurrection are not to be seen in isolation. From the moment we see the Cross, we see also the impending Resurrection. Thus the Cross is a symbol not of sorrow, but of joyful expectation. As we say at every Sunday Matins service:

Having seen the Resurrection of Christ, let us worship the Holy Lord Jesus, the only sinless one. We worship Your Cross, O Christ, and we

> *praise and glorify Your holy Resurrection. For You are our God; we know no other but You; we name You by name. Come, all the faithful, let us worship the holy Resurrection of Christ; for behold, through the Cross, joy has come into all the world. Ever blessing the Lord, we sing His Resurrection. For having endured the Cross for us, by death He has destroyed death. (Prayer after the reading of the Sunday Matins Gospel)*

Having thus been encouraged and inspired by the memory and veneration of the Cross on which Christ suffered for our sakes, we are persuaded to continue our own Lenten effort, to carry on bearing our cross for His sake, and to walk with our Lord to Calvary, that we may truly participate in the Passion, Death, and Resurrection of Christ. Only then, having followed Christ throughout the Lenten journey into Holy Week, will we truly be able to participate in the joy of His life-giving Resurrection.

↦ 11 ↤

The Canon of St. Andrew

CLEAN WEEK AND
THE FIFTH THURSDAY OF LENT

The end is at hand, my soul, is at hand! But you neither care nor prepare. The time is growing short. Arise! The Judge is at the door! Like a dream, like a flower, the time of this life passes. Why do we bustle about in vain? (Fourth ode of the Canon of St. Andrew)

As we saw in chapter two, the central theme of Lent is repentance. This theme is at the heart of one of the best-loved texts of Great Lent, the Great Canon of St. Andrew of Crete.

This text is heard during the first week of Lent as part of Great Compline, in which an extract of the Canon is chanted each day. In the middle of the fifth week of Lent, the Canon is chanted in its entirety.

The Canon is a dialogue between the Christian and his soul. The central theme is the urgent exhortation to change one's life. Thus the Canon is repeated in its entirety toward the end of Lent. If by now we have not begun to repent, then now is the time.

The Church knows that repentance is not easy. Even the holy author of the Canon is persistently reminding himself of his lack of repentance, striving to persuade himself to change his ways. The Church invites us to make his words our own. It is never too late to repent, as we are reminded in the Paschal Sermon of St. John Chrysostom:

> *Have any wearied themselves with fasting? Let them now enjoy their payment. Has anyone*

labored since the first hour? Let him today receive his due. Did any come after the third hour? Let them feast with gratitude. Did any arrive after the sixth hour? Let them not hesitate: for there is no penalty. Did any delay until after the ninth hour? Let them approach without hesitating. Did any arrive only for the eleventh hour? Let them not fear because of their lateness: for the Lord is generous and receives the last as the first: He gives rest to the worker of the eleventh hour as to those of the first. He has pity on the latter, He cares for the former. He gives to the one, He is generous to the other. He accepts the work done, He welcomes the intention. He honors the achievement, He praises the purpose. (The Paschal Vigil Service)

Yet the time for repentance is ever at hand. We are urged not to put it off any longer. At the beginning of Holy Week we hear the hymn:

Behold, the Bridegroom comes at midnight, and blessed is the servant whom He shall find watching. And again, unworthy is the servant

whom He shall find heedless. Beware, therefore, O my soul, do not be weighed down with sleep, lest you be given up to death, and lest you be shut out of the kingdom. But rouse yourself, crying, "Holy, holy, holy are You, our God."
(First troparion of Matins, Great and Holy Monday)

This hymn is based on the parable of the ten virgins (Matt. 25:1–13), which is a parable about the readiness of the soul to meet its Maker: "Behold, the bridegroom is coming; go out to meet him!" (Matt. 25:6).

In the Canon of St. Andrew, we are reminded that death is always at the door, and Christ, the Bridegroom of the Church, is near. Are you ready to meet Him? "Repent, for the kingdom of heaven is at hand" (Matt. 3:2).

12

Journey to Pascha

Desiring to commune with the Divine Pascha ... let us pursue victory over the devil through fasting. (First hymn of the aposticha for Vespers, Thursday of the first week of Lent)

From the middle of Lent, the Sunday of the Cross, we begin to see our journey's end, and the radiant feast of the Resurrection comes into view. Lent is a journey to Pascha. It is thus a season of joyful expectation. If we take Lent seriously, the journey is arduous, but this only makes Pascha all the more radiant and joyful. But throughout Lent, we are never allowed to forget the Resurrection, which fills all things, all ascetic labors, all solemnity, sorrow, and contrition, with gladness and brightness.

It would be a mistake to think of the sacrifices of Lent in purely negative terms—in terms of struggle and deprivation. We are to think of Lent as liberation. Lent calls us to sacrifice many of those things which, while they tend to occupy such a central position in our lives, while they seem to us to be so important, are in reality things we can do without. Lent is thus the rediscovery of that which is most essential in our lives. In this rediscovery, we return to God and to the very meaning of life.

Thus, having stripped ourselves of all that is petty and futile, having cast off the burdensome baggage of our worldly and often complex lifestyles, we can truly experience Lent as liberation and purification, as the necessary, fruitful, and wonderful journey to the joy of Pascha.

About the Author

ARCHIMANDRITE Vassilios Papavassiliou is a priest of the Greek Orthodox Archdiocese of Thyateira and Great Britain. He was born in London in 1977 and holds degrees in pastoral and social theology, classics, and Byzantine music. He is the author of *Journey to the Kingdom: An Insider's Look at the Liturgy and Beliefs of the Eastern Orthodox Church* (Paraclete Press) and numerous articles on Christian Orthodox faith and theology.

Other Books from Conciliar Press

Bread & Water, Wine & Oil
by Archimandrite Meletios Webber

According to two thousand years of experience, Orthodoxy shows us how to be transformed by the renewing of our mind—a process that is aided by participation in the traditional ascetic practices and Mysteries of the Church. In this unique and accessible book, Archimandrite Meletios Webber first explores the role of mystery in the Christian life, then walks the reader through the seven major Mysteries of the Orthodox Church, showing the way to a richer, fuller life in Christ.

A Beginner's Guide to Spirituality
by Michael Keiser

Fr. Michael Keiser walks us through the Orthodox Church's timeless teachings and practices on the ancient understanding of Christian spirituality with humor and keen insight. He outlines how ascetic practices, personal and corporate worship, confession and repentance, overcoming the passions, and opening ourselves up to God's grace can lead us to transformation, and to our ultimate destiny—Jerusalem, the heavenly city.

The Scent of Holiness
by Constantina Palmer
Every monastery exudes the scent of holiness, but women's monasteries have their own special flavor. Join Constantina Palmer as she makes frequent pilgrimages to a women's monastery in Greece and absorbs the nuns' particular approach to their spiritual life. If you're a woman who's read of Mount Athos and longed to partake of its grace-filled atmosphere, this book is for you. Men will find it a fascinating read as well.

A Book of Hours
by Patricia Colling Egan
Eastern and Western Christians share a rich spiritual heritage in the Hours of Prayer—the brief services of praise and psalmody that mark the progress of each day, sanctifying the hours of our lives. In this gem of a book, Patricia Egan digs deeply into the meaning of each of the Hours, drawing on poetry, nature, experience, and theology to show how the services reflect the different aspects of our salvation and our lives. *A Book of Hours* is an excellent companion for anyone who wants to experience the blessing of praying through the Hours of each day.

All titles available at www.conciliarpress.com. Most also available as ebooks.